RUGBY WORLD CUP

GLOBAL CITIZENS: SPORTS

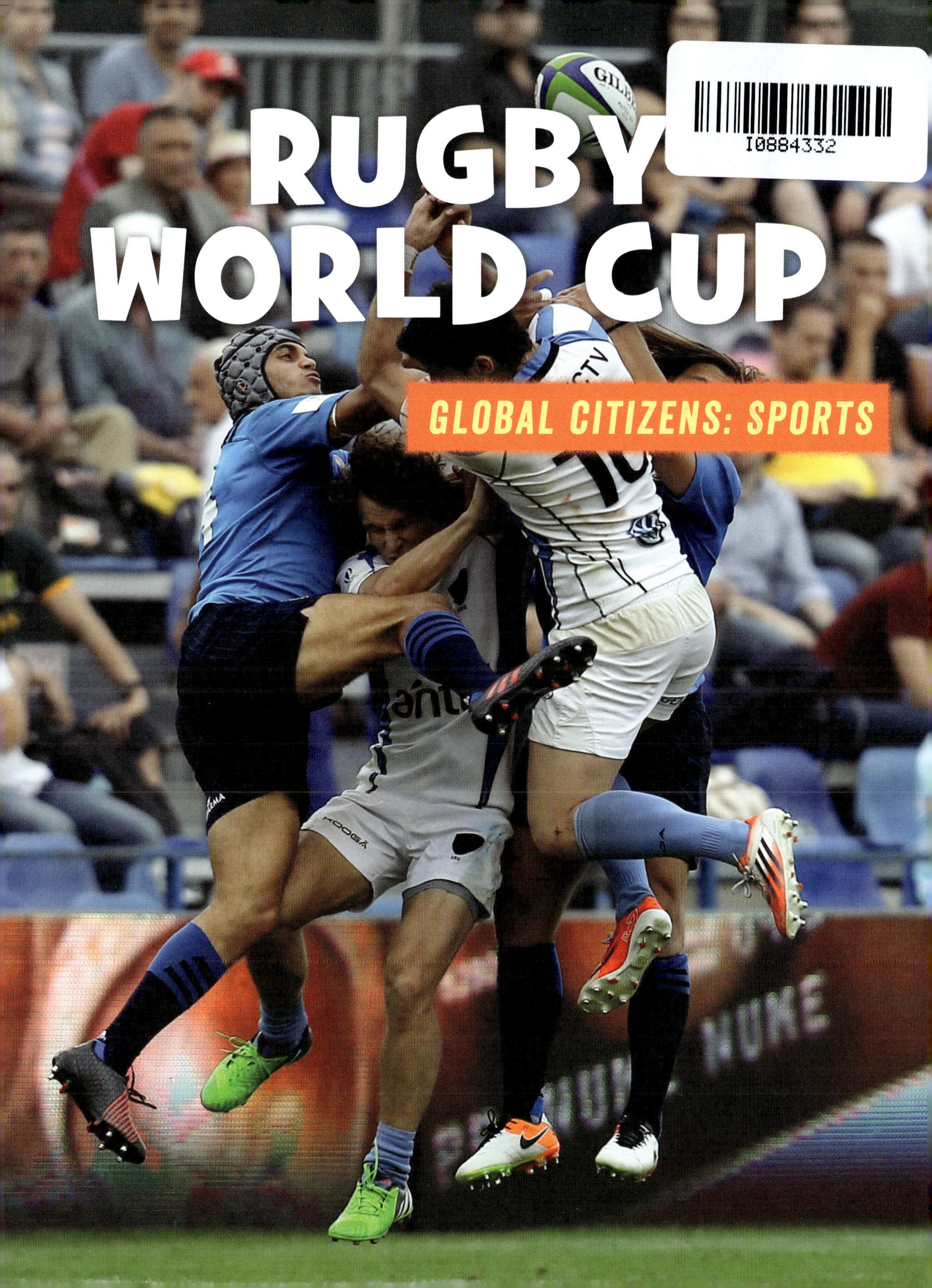

Published in the United States of America by Cherry Lake Publishing
Ann Arbor, Michigan
www.cherrylakepublishing.com

Content Adviser: Liv Williams, Editor, www.iLivExtreme.com
Reading Adviser: Marla Conn, MS, Ed., Literacy specialist, Read-Ability, Inc.

Photo Credits: ©Guy Bell/Alamy Stock Photo, cover; ©Stef22/Dreamstime, 1; ©Paolo Bona/Shutterstock, 5; ©Kevin Richards/Shutterstock, 6; ©fstockfoto/Shutterstock, 7; ©Paolo Bona/Shutterstock, 8; ©Mitch Gunn/Shutterstock, 11; ©Paolo Bona/Shutterstock, 13; ©Grosremy/Dreamstime, 14; ©Mark Eaton/Dreamstime, 17; ©Patrimonio Designs Limited/Dreamstime, 18; ©Mai Groves/Shutterstock, 19; ©salajean/Shutterstock, 20; ©Luke Schmidt/Dreamstime, 21; ©Mehmet Dilsiz/Shutterstock, 22; ©Chun Yip Leung/Dreamstime, 23; ©Ned Snowman/Shutterstock, 24; ©Urban Napflin/Shutterstock, 27; ©Tooykrub/Shutterstock, 28

Library of Congress Cataloging-in-Publication Data

Names: Hellebuyck, Adam, author. | Deimel, Laura, author.
Title: Rugby World Cup / written by Adam Hellebuyck and Laura Deimel.
Description: Ann Arbor, Michigan : Cherry Lake Publishing, [2019] | Series: Global Citizens: Sports | Audience: Grades 4 to 6 | Includes bibliographical references and index.
Identifiers: LCCN 2019004214 | ISBN 9781534147515 (hardcover) | ISBN 9781534150379 (paperback) | ISBN 9781534148949 (pdf) | ISBN 9781534151802 (hosted ebook)
Subjects: LCSH: World Cup (Rugby football)—Juvenile literature.
Classification: LCC GV945.5 .H45 2019 | DDC 796.333/65—dc23
LC record available at https://lccn.loc.gov/2019004214

Cherry Lake Publishing would like to acknowledge the work of the Partnership for 21st Century Learning. Please visit *www.p21.org* for more information.

Printed in the United States of America
Corporate Graphics

ABOUT THE AUTHORS

Laura Deimel is a fourth grade teacher and Adam Hellebuyck is a high school social studies teacher at University Liggett School in Grosse Pointe Woods, Michigan. They have worked together for the past 8 years and are thrilled they could combine two of their passions, reading and sports, into this work.

TABLE OF CONTENTS

CHAPTER 1

History: The Beginning

Rugby has a long and exciting history as a sport. Teams from over 100 countries compete to enter the Rugby World Cup. The World Cup has been held every 4 years since 1987 to determine which country has the best team.

The Origins of Rugby

In 1823, students at Rugby School, an educational institution for boys, were playing soccer. They changed the rules of soccer to allow players to carry the ball with their hands instead of just kicking it with their feet. There is a legend that the first rugby player was a student named William Webb Ellis, but there is little evidence that this is true. Over time, the game became more

The winners receive the Webb Ellis Cup, which is named after the legendary founder of rugby, William Webb Ellis.

Rugby is the only major sport named after the place it was created instead of how it is played. It is named after the Rugby School in Rugby, Warwickshire, England.

popular at schools around England, even colleges. But there were no formal rules—teams would meet before a game to decide the rules they would play by. By 1845, the game had grown so popular that one set of rules needed to be written.

Rugby Union and Rugby League

Over time, rugby divided into rugby football, rugby league, and rugby union. Rugby football evolved into the game we know today as American football. Rugby league and rugby union

For the first few decades, rugby balls were made from a pig's bladder!

According to surveys, the Rugby World Cup is the world's third most popular sporting event after the Olympics and the FIFA World Cup.

divided in 1895 when rugby leaders disagreed on what the rules should be for the game. Rugby league rules are designed to make the game faster and are believed to be simpler than the rules of rugby union. The rugby union rules are more **traditional** and complex. While rugby league is more popular in Australia, rugby union is more popular around the world. The Rugby World Cup is played by the rules of the rugby union.

The World Cup

Rugby competitions have been held since 1882, when the Four Nations Cup began between England, Scotland, Ireland, and Wales. However, teams from elsewhere around the world didn't compete against each other until 1987, when the Rugby World Cup was created. Before this, many teams did not want to have a global competition. Sixteen countries participated in the first Rugby World Cup, with New Zealand defeating France to become the first champions.

Developing Questions

Over time, rugby union and rugby league began to look different because of their different rules. If you could interview a rugby union player and a rugby league player, what questions would you ask them to learn about all the differences in how they play the game? Share these questions with your friends, family, or teachers who are interested in rugby. How else could you find answers to these questions?

CHAPTER 2

Geography: Rugby Worldwide

Rugby began in England but is now played all over the world. There are teams in over 100 countries that compete to enter the Rugby World Cup tournament. Each of these countries and teams has a different story.

Japan

The 2019 Rugby World Cup will be held in Japan. This is the first time a tournament will take place in Asia. Over 2.5 million people from around the world have requested to buy tickets for all the matches—a record number! About 70 percent of those people are from outside Japan. The tournament is expected to bring a lot of money to the Japanese economy.

Japan has about 125,000 registered rugby players and more than 3,600 rugby clubs.

The Japanese national team is called the Cherry Blossoms. This is also the name of the country's national flower and represents the cycle of life and death. Every year, Japan holds a festival in the spring to view the beautiful cherry blossoms as they bloom. The Cherry Blossoms have played in every Rugby World Cup tournament since it began.

Australia and New Zealand

Rugby has been played in Australia since 1864 and is very popular. There are nearly 90,000 registered rugby players in the country. The Australian national team is nicknamed the Wallabies. The Wallabies have won the Rugby World Cup twice, in 1991 and 1999, and are usually ranked among the top teams in the sport each year.

New Zealand, which is near Australia, also has a long history with the sport of rugby. In fact, rugby is New Zealand's national sport. The country's team is called the All Blacks. The team is named for their uniforms, which are completely black. The All Blacks team has won the Rugby World Cup three times: in 1987, 2011, and 2015. The All Blacks are known for performing a *haka*, which is a **ritual** dance, at the beginning of their games. The dance is part of the Māori culture. The Māori are **indigenous** to New Zealand, much like Native Americans are indigenous to the United States.

New Zealand's All Blacks team has won the most World Cup games since 1987.

South Africa

South Africa hosted the Rugby World Cup in 1995. At that time, the country had just ended apartheid, a system where the government **discriminated** against black people in favor of white people. But black and white people were still divided. During the 1995 Rugby World Cup, all members of the country **rallied** around the South African national team, the Springboks. The Springboks are named after a type of deer that lives in

Several movies, such as *The 16th Man* and *Invictus*, have been made about the final match in the 1995 Rugby World Cup and its importance to South Africa.

southern Africa. When the Springboks defeated New Zealand in the finals to win the Rugby World Cup, South African president Nelson Mandela went onto the **pitch** to congratulate the team. The whole country celebrated this important championship, which started to bring blacks and whites together as one country.

Gathering and Evaluating Sources

While over 100 countries compete to qualify for the Rugby World Cup tournament, some countries are more successful than others. Take a look at a list of the countries that have qualified for every Rugby World Cup tournament since they began. What do you notice about these countries geographically? Why do you think these teams have qualified for the tournament more than others? Using your local library and the internet, try to figure it out!

Argentina
Australia
Canada
England
France
Ireland
Italy
Japan
New Zealand
Romania
Scotland
Wales

CHAPTER 3

Civics: Reasons for the Rules

Rules are very important in the sport of rugby, especially when teams are competing for the World Cup. There are very specific rules on how teams can get the ball, how to score points, and how the game should be played safely. The game is played on a pitch, which has goal lines for each team and vertical posts that players can kick the ball through, like in American football.

Interesting Plays

Rugby is a unique game because the ball can only be passed backward, not forward down the pitch. This all happens while the players are moving forward. If the ball is passed forward, the referee will stop the match and call for a scrummage, or scrum for short. A scrum is a restart of the game. In a scrum,

Rugby players are expected to show respect for the referee's decisions at all times. They argue much less with officials than in other sports.

The 2015 World Cup introduced a new set of scrum rules to help reduce the number of injuries.

eight players from each team stand in specific spots and form one huddle. The ball is then tossed into the middle of the scrum. The players can only touch the ball with their feet. They use their feet in order to move the ball backward until it exits at the back of the scrum. Only then can either team pick up the ball again to pass.

Scoring Points

In order to win the Rugby World Cup, teams need to score more points than their opponents. There are many ways to score points in rugby. A try is scored when the ball is carried past an

For the most part, the rules for the Women's Rugby World Cup are the same as the men's.

Experts believe that even qualifying for the World Cup can strengthen a nation's identity.

The First National Bank Stadium in South Africa can seat almost 10,000 fans.

opponent's goal line. A try is worth five points. The team that scores a try can also attempt a conversion. A conversion is worth two points and is scored when a player kicks the ball through the two vertical posts on the pitch. Players can also score a drop goal if they kick the ball through the posts at any time they are on offense. A drop goal is worth three points.

While most rugby games can end in a tie, which is called a draw, games in the World Cup are an exception to that rule. This is because one team needs to win in order to move on in the tournament.

Some players wear scrum caps to protect their ears. Researchers believe it helps make the sport 47 percent safer.

Protecting the Players

While players can tackle each other in rugby, there are fewer serious injuries in this sport than in others, like soccer and football. Many people think this is because players do not wear a lot of protective padding. Rugby officials believe that if players wore lots of padding and other protective gear, like helmets, they might use those against other players. They believe that without a lot of padding, players might not hit each other as hard. The only protective gear required for a rugby player is a mouth guard.

Mouth guards help protect players against injuries like concussions and teeth-related injuries.

To respect Japanese culture, the 2019 World Cup players were asked to cover up tattoos when in public settings.

However, some players have started wearing a soft head guard to protect their ears from being injured.

There are very specific rules for how players can tackle each other in rugby. A player is only allowed to tackle the person carrying the ball and must grab that player below the shoulders. After tackling an opponent, a player must let go of that person as soon as they are on the ground, to prevent injury. Any player who does not follow these rules for tackling is given a serious penalty by the match official.

Developing Claims and Using Evidence

There is a chance that players can get injured during a match. The common types of rugby injuries and how frequently they happen are listed in the chart below:

Type of Injury	Percent of Total Injuries
Bruises	*40*
Muscle sprains (including sprained ankles)	*30*
Concussions	*10*

Research the types of injuries listed above and think about how these might happen in a rugby match. Using the information you found, think about how you might change the game to keep these injuries from happening.

CHAPTER 4

Economics: Jerseys Sell

The teams in the Rugby World Cup often wear colorful uniforms covered with all kinds of images and writing. Team jerseys are an important way that rugby organizations make money to play in the World Cup.

Colors Make Money

Team colors are a source of pride for fans. These colors can be found on all kinds of **merchandise** related to the teams. For example, the South African Springboks' colors are green and gold. Springboks supporters can buy all kinds of items in these

An estimated 400,000 fans will travel to Japan from all over the world during the 2019 World Cup.

colors, such as shoes, T-shirts, hats, scarves, rugby match balls, dog collars, and key chains! These items help pay for national teams to enter the Rugby World Cup.

Jersey Sponsorship

In addition to selling products in their jersey colors, teams have **sponsorships** on their jerseys that earn them money. Teams sell locations on their jerseys, such as the sleeves or the chest, to companies that want to advertise their products.

Experts believe that Japan might see as much as a $3.5-billion boost in economic activity for hosting the 2019 World Cup.

The center of the jersey is the most **coveted** location for a sponsorship. For example, the New Zealand All Blacks did

Taking Informed Action

Rugby is gaining popularity all over the world. Think about the area where you live and if there is a rugby team nearby. If not, how could you start your own rugby group? What would you need to do? How could you raise money to get the supplies you need? Using your local library and the internet, explore how to start a rugby club at your school or in your neighborhood.

not have a sponsor in the center of their jerseys for a long time. When they finally decided to add a sponsor in 2012, the company AIG paid $80 million to have that spot. Selling sponsorships on jerseys can make rugby teams a lot of money.

Selling Team Jerseys

Rugby teams can also make a lot of money by selling their jerseys, especially during the Rugby World Cup. Fans can purchase **replicas** of what the players wear in their matches. These replicas can sell for over $200 each for popular teams like the New Zealand All Blacks. While this might seem like a lot of money, the cost of designing the jersey, printing it, shipping it from the factory, and taxes can raise its price.

Communicating Conclusions

Selling sponsorships on jerseys can make rugby teams a lot of money, which they can use to travel to the World Cup or spend on supplies they need. Think about the sports teams at your school. Would you like to find a sponsor for one of your school teams? If so, what would the benefits be? Are there any negatives to having a sponsor? If you added a sponsor to one of your sports teams, where would you put that sponsorship on the team jerseys and why?

Think About It

Each national team that participates in the Rugby World Cup has a nickname. Many of these nicknames are animals in their countries or related to their team colors. Take a look at the list of team nicknames below. Using the internet and your local library, try to figure out how the team nickname is connected to that country. Share what you found with your friends!

Country	Team Nickname
Algeria	The Lion Cubs
Argentina	The Pumas
Belgium	The Black Devils
Cambodia	The Buffalos
France	The 15 of France
Kenya	The Simbas
The Netherlands	The Orange
Pakistan	The Greenshirts
Poland	The White-Reds
Russia	The Bears

For More Information

Further Reading

Jones, Emma. *Girls Play Rugby.* New York, NY: PowerKids Press, 2017.

Mason, Paul. *Be a Rugby Expert.* London: Franklin Watts, 2017.

Websites

Rugby World Cup
https://www.rugbyworldcup.com
Learn more about the World Cup at the official website.

YouTube—Rugby World Cup 1995: New Zealand vs South Africa
https://www.youtube.com/watch?v=LmQHWex_UFo
Watch the famous 1995 Rugby World Cup finals match played in Ellis Park Stadium, Johannesburg, South Africa, between New Zealand and South Africa.

GLOSSARY

coveted (KUHV-it-id) desired

discriminated (dis-KRIM-uh-nate-id) treated someone unfairly

indigenous (in-DIJ-uh-nuhs) native

merchandise (MUR-chun-dise) items to be bought or sold

pitch (PICH) the playing field for rugby

rallied (RAL-eed) to come together in support

replicas (REP-lih-kuhz) an exact copy of something

ritual (RICH-oo-uhl) an activity that has specific actions that need to be done in a certain order

sponsorships (SPAHN-sur-ships) when a company gives an organization money to advertise its products

traditional (truh-DISH-uh-nuhl) having been done the same way for a long time

INDEX